TO:

_____

FROM:

_____

THIS IS GOD

PHIL VASSAR

RUTLEDGE HILL PRESS®

Nashville, Tennessee

A DIVISION OF THOMAS NELSON, INC.

www.ThomasNelson.com

To all my family and friends
whom I see God work through every day.

Published by Rutledge Hill Press, a Division of Thomas Nelson, Inc.,
P.O. Box 141000, Nashville, Tennessee 37214.

Photo credits: Front & back endsheets, pages 12, 19, 31 licensed through Corbis Images. Page 4: Glenn Rose/BMI.
Frontispiece, pages 4, 9, 24, 46, 53, 54, 62/63 licensed through Getty Images. Pages 38/39, 43 licensed through Creatas
Images. Page 44 licensed through SuperStock.

Cover & text design by Bruce Gore / Gore Studio, Inc.

ISBN: 1-4016-0120-0

Printed in the United States of America

03 04 05 06 — 6 5 4 3 2

THIS IS GOD

Hey, this is God.
Could I please have your attention?
There's a need for intervention.
Man, I'm disappointed in what
    I'm seeing.
Yeah, this is God.
You fight each other in my name,
Treat life like it's a foolish game.
I say you've got the wrong idea.

Oh, all I'm asking for is love.
I've seen you hurt yourselves enough.
Oh, I've been waiting for a change
    in you.

Yeah, this is God.
I've given everything to you.
Oh, but look at what you do
To the world that I created.
This is God.
What's with this attitude and hate?
You grow more ignorant with age.

You had it made, now look at all
    you've wasted.

All I'm asking for is love.
I've seen you hurt yourselves enough.
Oh, I've been waiting on a change
    in you.

I know your every thought, your heart
    and soul and every move.
There are so many consequences
    to the things you do.

Oh, all I'm asking for is love.
Haven't you hurt yourselves enough?
Oh, I've been waiting for a change
    in you,

Change in you.

This is God.

Nот тоо LONG AGO I was on an airplane, reading a newspaper about all the things going on in the world. Alone in my window seat, I found myself staring into the clouds. My mind began to drift, wondering if God must look down on us with disappointment. One thought led to another and I began writing what became the song "This Is God." I safely tucked it away in my notepad and nodded off to sleep. Soon after returning to Nashville, I was in the studio recording some new songs, and almost in passing recorded a version of "This is God." I never expected it to be recorded on an album, much less released as a single to radio. The response has amazed and astounded me. This book is simply an attempt to put down all the thoughts that came to me that day on the airplane—the things I thought God might say to us.

Let me state right here that I do not feel qualified to put words into God's mouth. When you write a song, there are many thoughts and lines that come to mind that can't make the final version because you just cannot do anything with a ten-minute song. This book shares those thoughts. Some are whimsical, some a little more serious, but I hope they give you insight into the things that were running through my head when I wrote the song. More importantly, I hope this book helps you appreciate everything and everyone you have in your life.

—PHIL VASSAR

REMEMBER
THIS...

ALL
I'M ASKING FOR IS
LOVE.

I put you here for a REASON.

Your
life

MATTERS.

DON'T LET MONEY BE YOUR GOD.

It will never love you as I do.

Have faith in Me.

There is hope.

Leave the world a **BETTER PLACE** than it was before you arrived.

ALWAYS FIGHT EVIL

BE HAPPY FOR THE SUCCESS OF OTHERS.

LEARN
from the past;

PREPARE
for the future;

FOCUS
on the present.

BEND A LITTLE.

YOU'RE
NOT
ALWAYS RIGHT.

LAUGH

uncontrollably.

LOVE

unconditionally.

DON'T CAUSE CONFUSION.

DON'T BE BOASTFUL.

DON'T HURT OTHERS.

Build bridges.

Envy

won't bring you satisfaction.

MIRACLES
really do
HAPPEN.

I GAVE YOU THE MOON, THE EARTH, THE STARS, AND MY SON.

KEEP
YOUR PROMISES.

~

TELL
THE TRUTH.

Admire nature.
IT'S BEAUTIFUL.

SHOW OTHERS you know Me.

FORGIVE

It's HARDER *than forgiving others.*

YOURSELF.

Remember that I forgive FREELY.

GIVE *with a* GENEROUS SPIRIT.

FIGHT FOR YOUR FREEDOM.

And stand up for the freedom of those who cannot fight for themselves.

CHASE
*your dreams
with all your*
HEART.

BE WILLING TO CHANGE.

___

AND WHEN YOU'VE CHANGED, BE WILLING TO CHANGE AGAIN.

YOU ARE NOT ALONE.

TAKE GOOD CARE OF YOUR BODY.

You can't have another one.

THINK
BEFORE YOU
SPEAK.

Choose your friends

WISELY.

Pray for your enemies.

CALL
your parents.

KISS
your children.

HONOR
your spouse.

DON'T GIVE UP.

You can
please Me
by being
JUST.

*You can show
you love Me
through*

RIGHTEOUS-NESS.

I love to hear you

SING

OUT LOUD.

IT'S OK TO BREAK THE RULES.

Just don't break MINE.

DON'T
BE AFRAID.

DON'T
WORRY.

Put your trust in Me.

Take advantage of every minute you're given.

Be *passionate* about your family.

*Treat
each other
with*

RESPECT.

EMBRACE EACH SUNRISE.

⟨⟩⟨⟩⟨⟩

CHERISH EVERY SUNSET.

REMEMBER, YOU'RE NOT PERFECT.

——— ⌇⌇⌇ ———

ONLY I CAN SAY THAT.

REACH

for

HEAVEN.

STOP BEING UNHAPPY.

HAPPINESS IS A CHOICE.

Be thankful.

Choose the

HIGH ROAD.

If someone is hungry,
give him
FOOD.

If someone is thirsty,
give him something to
DRINK.

I made every one of you to be different.

ENJOY
IT.

TAKE CARE OF THE EARTH.

What you see
is all you've got.

LIVE

by my

WORD.

Be a GOOD FRIEND.

BE
CAREFUL
how you use
My name.

I will never leave you.

―◦◦◦―

IF IT SEEMS I'M DISTANT, ASK YOURSELF WHO'S MOVED— YOU OR ME?

DON'T SETTLE FOR BEING

GOOD ENOUGH.

Don't be so
SERIOUS.

KNOWLEDGE
is power:

KINDNESS
is even more powerful.

I'm repeating myself, but...

I put you here for a

REASON.

I'm ready to listen

WHENEVER YOU'RE READY TO TALK.

ALL
I'M ASKING
FOR
IS LOVE.

I love you.

—God.